Perfect
PRESERVES

Perfect PRESERVES

Easy Recipes for Delicious Jams, Jellies, Pickles, and Relishes

M. Dalton King

Photography by Zeva Oelbaum

SMITHMARK

A FRIEDMAN GROUP BOOK

© 1994 by Michael Friedman Publishing Group, Inc.
All photographs ©Zeva Oelbaum

This edition published in 1994 by SMITHMARK Publishers Inc.
16 East 32nd Street, New York NY 10016.

SMITHMARK Books are available for bulk purchase for sales promotion and premium use. For details write or call the manager of special sales, SMITHMARK Publishers Inc., 16 East 32nd Street, New York, NY 10016; (212) 532-6600.

PERFECT PRESERVES
Easy Recipes for Delicious Jams, Jellies, Pickles, and Relishes
was prepared and produced by
Michael Friedman Publishing Group, Inc.
15 West 26th Street
New York, NY 10010

Editor: Nathaniel Marunas
Art Director: Jeff Batzli
Designer: Susan E. Livingston
Photography Director: Christopher C. Bain
Food Stylist: Kathy Blake
Prop Stylist: Lynn McMahill
Handmade Raku pottery by Fred Rose for Chelsea Ceramic Guild, New York City

Library of Congress Cataloging-in-Publication Data

King, M. Dalton.
    Perfect preserves : easy recipes for delicious jams, jellies, pickles,
and relishes/M. Dalton King ; photography by Zeva Oelbaum.
        p. cm.
    ISBN 0-8317-1102-7 : $9.98
    1. Canning and preserving. I. Title.
TX601.K55 1994
641.4'2—dc20   93-33782
                                                                  CIP

Color separations by Universal Colour Scanning Ltd.
Printed and bound in China by Leefung-Asco Printers Ltd.

10 9 8 7 6 5 4 3 2 1

Dedication

To Mary Lou Alberts, a.k.a. Merle,
with great love, affection, and thanks.

Contents

Introduction

Recently, while on a trip to Philadelphia, I took the opportunity to visit that city's Reading Terminal Market. The Terminal Market is an enormous indoor food court where you can find the very freshest of meats and produce, homemade ice cream, just-baked bread, barbecue, deli, big fat pretzels, and just about anything else you can imagine. As I wandered past the individual stalls and spaces, I noticed a lot of activity occurring at one counter in particular, a few aisles over. Curious, I headed in that direction and came upon Amish women selling their homemade pickles, jams, and relishes. That these items were in great demand I could well understand. Home-cooked preserves and canned goods have come back in vogue over the past decade. People have once again begun to recognize the high quality and superior taste of foods prepared at home.

There is good reason for this. People are more likely to take greater care and time when choosing and preparing fruits and vegetables for their family than a manufacturer would for mass distribution. Homemade preserves are chemical free, and the amount of fresh fruit in jams, conserves, chutneys, and the like is greater than in those offered by your friendly neighborhood market. And if you are fortunate enough to have a garden, the merits of home preserving are obvious. You will be following a centuries-old tradition of "putting food by" against the time when nature withdraws her bounty in the great annual freeze.

A further incentive for delving into the world of preserves is that they make splendid and valued gifts. Now, instead of bringing flowers to a dinner party, I present decorated jars of my latest efforts to my (very appreciative) hosts. One Christmas I sent jars of peach preserves and strawberry sauce to those to whom I wished to extend the greetings of the season. All the thank-you notes expressed a desire to be placed on next year's list.

In this book I will provide you with the basics, the how-to's of canning and preserving. I will describe the principles behind preserving and all the methods available so that you will have a firm understanding of why and when certain steps need to be taken to ensure safe storage of the food prepared. I tell you about pressure canning, even though it's a method I never use. (I don't need to: the availability of grocery stores with an abundance of food makes it unnecessary for me to store meats and whole vegetables.) Just the same, I feel that it is best before starting any new endeavor to have a complete picture because it allows you to make informed choices. Of course, I also give you a variety of recipes I think you'll enjoy serving. Using the guidelines provided, you should not only be able to prepare the recipes in this book, but make changes to suit your family's taste or even create rewarding and delicious recipes of your own.

Preserving takes care and patience, but is well worth the effort. As you place the fruits of your labor on your table months after you have done the work, I guarantee you will feel a glow of satisfaction and pride for a job well and lovingly done.

CHAPTER ONE

The Basics

In times past, food was kept for future use by means such as smoking, drying, salting, and simply storing it in a cold, dark place (a root cellar, for instance). Preserving as we know it didn't begin to happen until the early part of the nineteenth century, and even then the method was haphazard and the results not at all foolproof. As time progressed, methods improved, and by the end of the century, cans were a familiar convenience. Putting up home preserves had become an annual spring and summer ritual. Today, with the convenience of modern stoves, refrigerators, freezers, pressure canners, and microwaves, it is much easier to achieve safe results. It is, however, necessary to understand the principles of canning and why the methods suggested in this book are employed.

The Principles

Preserving is, to put it simply, a means of storing food, both cooked and "raw," against a future date. To do this, you have to seal the food in an airtight container and process it in such a way that the four main spoilers—enzymes, molds, yeasts, and bacteria—are eliminated and do not render your food unsafe to eat. Three things will retard or prevent the growth of these spoilers: heat, cold, and the introduction of acidity into the product.

HEAT

The introduction of heat—high heat—into the canning process kills the enzymes and bacteria, eliminates the air, and provides an airtight container, which prevents the growth of molds and yeast. Heat is used in the open-kettle, water bath, pressure canner, microwave, and steamer methods of processing.

COLD

Working in the opposite direction of heat, freezing your preserves provides an atmosphere in which the various spoilers are frozen into dormancy and thus are unable to grow and propagate.

ACIDITY

The acidity of the food you are preserving will be a major factor in determining which processing method to use when putting up your preserves. Most food, with the exception of fruit and tomatoes, has a high pH factor and thus is low in natural acid. The balance can be redressed with the addition of vinegar, lemon juice, or citric acid. (My preference has always been to use vinegar or lemon juice; it's simpler, and I know exactly what I'm dealing with.) The combination of acidity and heat will provide you with safe preserves. If acidity is low or absent, by either nature's design or your choice, higher heat and greater pressure will have to be used when the food is processed.

Methods of Preparation and Preserving

Cold (or raw) pack is a preparation method whereby raw fresh fruit and vegetables are firmly packed into clean, hot jars, covered with a hot or boiling liquid such as water or syrup, sealed, and processed using one of the methods listed below. For maximum safety, cold-packed foods should be processed in a water bath or pressure canner.

Hot pack is a method in which cooked or partially cooked hot food is packed into clean, hot, sterilized jars, sealed, and processed by one of the methods listed below.

The open-kettle method is quite the easiest of the lot and works best when used to prepare jams, jellies, marmalades, butters, conserves, and some relishes, condiments, and pickles. To process using the open-kettle method, the food must first be cooked in either a vinegar or a sugar base (or a combination of the two). You then pour the hot food into clean, hot, sterilized jars, leaving the appropriate amount of headroom. Wipe the rim of the jar clean of any food or juice using a clean, damp cloth, and seal the jars firmly but not excessively tight. Turn the jars over and let them sit for ten minutes. The heat of the food will seal the lid and create the vacuum needed for safe food storage. Turning the jars over in this way is called the inversion method. After the ten minutes are up, return the jars to an upright position and let them sit on wire racks or dish towels, approximately two inches apart, until cool. Check your lids to see that they are airtight. Label each jar with the name, date, and expected shelf life, and store in a cool, dry place. The expected shelf life for foods processed in this way is one year.

The water bath method is used when processing whole fruit, acidic vegetables, some condiments, relishes, chutneys, and most tomato products.

To use the water bath method, you need a large stainless steel or enameled cooking pot that is wide enough to hold the jars you wish to process without crowding them (the jars must not touch) and deep enough that the jars will be completely submerged in water with two to three inches of water above them. You will also need to put a rack on the bottom of the pot upon which the jars can sit without coming too close to the source of heat. You can buy a water bath canner (complete with rack) at your local hardware or housewares store.

To process, fill clean, hot jars with the food, leaving the appropriate amount of headroom. Remove air bubbles by running a rubber spatula around the edge of the food. Clean the rim of each jar using a clean, damp cloth. Place the lids, twisting firmly but not tightly.

Place the jars in the water bath, making sure the jars are covered by two to three inches of water, and bring to a boil. Once the boil has commenced, start counting off the processing time required in your recipe. When the jars have been processed, use a pair of tongs to lift the jars out, one at a time, and place them on clean dish towels. Invert the jars carefully and leave them for ten minutes. This inversion is an excellent way of testing your seals and ensuring that your jars are airtight. Set the jars upright, about two inches apart, and allow them to cool away from drafts. Label each jar and store in a cool, dry place. The shelf life of food processed in a water bath is one year.

Pressure canning is used to preserve most vegetables, poultry, meat, and fish. A pressure canner is a pot that has a lid that clamps tightly shut, and comes equipped with a weight gauge, a vent from which the steam escapes (called a petcock), and a safety pressure valve, which controls the amount of pressure in the canner.

To use the pressure canner, fill clean, hot jars with the food you wish to preserve, wipe the rims with a clean, damp cloth, and seal as you would for the water bath method. Once your jars are ready, proceed as instructed by the manufacturer of your pressure canner. It is important that you follow the instructions exactly. When you have finished processing, cool your jars, label them, and store them in a cool, dry place.

Freezing is an easy and convenient way of preserving food. In fact, I prefer this method for vegetables; they taste fresher, in my opinion. This method is best for food that will be able to withstand the freezing process and subsequent thawing. Pickles, chutneys, and relishes would not be good candidates for freezing, while fruit and vegetables, such as corn and green beans, would. To use this method optimally, it is necessary for your fruit and vegetables to be very fresh and of the very highest quality.

To preserve by freezing, fill sterilized containers with the fresh food, leaving one inch headroom to accommodate the expansion that occurs during freezing. Remove excess air bubbles by running a spatula around the edge of the food, wipe the rims clean, and seal with airtight lids. Label the jars using indelible or water-resistant pens and freeze immediately. Frozen foods have a shelf life of approximately six months.

Refrigeration is an excellent means of preservation when you are making only a small amount of food that you will keep for only a short period of time. Place your food in clean, sterilized jars, wipe the rims clean, cap tightly with lids, and refrigerate immediately. A week to ten days is the safest period of time in which to use this food.

Microwave preservation is starting to appear in books and articles. I consider it the canning method of the future. Microwave ovens are not yet temperature standardized enough for this method to be as effective as the open-kettle and water bath methods. Should you wish to experiment, do so, but remember that the jars will still have to be sterilized and you will still have to take the necessary steps for sealing the product.

Steaming and oven canning are methods I would discourage. When using the steaming method, the jars are placed in a canner, which allows steam to circulate around the jars. However, there can be problems with seepage and getting a proper seal, which makes me reluctant to use it.

Oven canning, on the other hand, can be downright dangerous. Oven heat is dry and not terribly effective, and there is the greatest possibility that when you remove the jars from the oven, they will explode. Enough said!

Headroom

Whenever you read a preserving recipe, you are generally told, or should be, to leave a certain amount of headroom. What exactly is it? Headroom is the air space between the food and the top of the jar. Whenever you preserve food, you must leave some room for the expansion that may occur during heating and will absolutely occur with freezing. Too little headroom will push the food to the top of the jar and offset the seal. Too much headroom may cause discoloration of the food and also affect proper sealing. Most recipes will tell you how much headroom to leave. If that information is missing, a good rule of thumb is to leave one-quarter inch headroom for foods that are cold packed and one-half inch for hot-packed foods.

Jars, Caps, and Sterilizing

When preserving, it is best, absolutely best, to use standard canning jars. They are widely available for purchase at reasonable prices in housewares, hardware, and variety stores. At the peak of canning season, some grocery stores even carry them. Additionally, specialty food catalogs offer decorated jars or ones that come with painted lids. The two types of jars I recommend are below.

• The can or freeze jar (commonly known as the Mason or Ball jar), which is made from tempered glass, able to withstand all temperatures, and available in a variety of sizes, such as half-pint, pint, and quart. It comes with a two-part metal cap that consists of a metal lid, which is lined in rubber, and a threaded frame, which screws over the lid and onto the jar.

• The lightning jar, which is available for canning use only. It comes with an attached dome lid, a rubber ring, which completes the seal, and a wire clamp to close the jar. It, too, comes in different sizes and should be available through the same sources as listed above.

To properly sterilize jars and caps, first wash them in hot, soapy water, rinse them, and then immerse them in a large pot of hot water. Bring the water to a boil and boil for ten minutes. Turn off the heat, but leave the jars in the hot water until ready for use. Using tongs, remove one jar and cap at a time. Fill each jar and cap it before removing another one. Should the water cool before you have a chance to use all the jars, bring the water to a boil again and proceed as instructed.

Equipment

When preserving, there is equipment you must have and equipment it would be nice to have. I'll tell you about both, along with the proviso that no matter what equipment you use, it is essential that it be spotlessly clean and free of rust, cracks, and chips.

NECESSARY:

Large stainless steel pot for cooking jams, jellies, chutneys, and the like

Large pot for sterilizing jars and caps

Large, heavy stainless steel or enameled pot with rack to use for a water bath

Food processor—wonderful help with preparation

Measuring cups and spoons

Long wooden spoon for stirring

Stainless steel slotted spoon

Wide-mouthed funnel

Ladle with pouring spout

Long rubber or plastic spatula for removing air from jars

Jar lifter or tongs

Strainer (a sieve or a colander covered in cheesecloth can be substituted)

Kitchen timer (many microwaves have a built-in timer, making it unnecessary to buy one)

Kitchen scale—useful when measuring exact amounts

Clean cloths

Proper jars

Labels

NICE TO HAVE:

Food mill—great for eliminating extra handwork

Wire racks—to place hot jars on for cooling

Jelly bag—makes jelly-making a cinch

Candy thermometer—good for indicating doneness

Preserving Step-by-Step

Now that you know the basics, how to sterilize your jars, and what equipment you need, the only thing left is to put them all together.

Before you start any canning project, some time should be taken for preparation. Preparation and preplanning are crucial to successful preserves. When you are in the midst of jam making, it is too late to discover that you don't have enough sugar. Sit down before starting, decide what you will make, and make sure you have all the ingredients, the equipment, and, most importantly, the time. Proper preserving cannot be interrupted for any length of time if you want to achieve successful results. There is no such thing as too much planning.

- Make sure that all surfaces, equipment, and anything else that comes into contact with the food are clean.

- Set out everything you will need so that the materials are close to hand the moment you need them.

- Begin by doing any food preparation that is necessary (peeling, chopping, and so on).

- Sterilize the jars and keep them hot.

- Cook the food (if necessary).

- Fill the jars, wipe the rims clean with a clean, damp cloth, and seal.

- Process the jars.

- Cool the jars (in a draft-free environment).

• Check the seals to make sure they are airtight.

• Label each jar with the name of the food, the date of preparation, and the expected shelf life.

• Store in a cool, dry place.

TIPS

Below are the little odds and ends of information that will help you achieve successful results.

• All fruits and vegetables should be fresh, of uniform size (if possible), and blemish-free.

• Do not double recipes; make each batch separately, one at a time.

• Do not use sugar substitutes; this discolors the fruit and causes a bitter aftertaste. Also, when sugar is called for it is often a necessary part of the preservation process.

• Use kosher salt rather than table salt when large quantities are called for.

• Never reuse metal lids.

• Spread your preserving over several days. This will cut down on fatigue, which results in mistakes.

• If you find you have leftovers (not quite enough to fill a jar) refrigerate and use over the next several days.

• If when you open your preserves you find abnormalities, such as mold or fizzy bubbles, or notice an odd smell, discard the contents immediately.

• If a seal is broken, discard the contents.

• Fill and seal the jars one at a time rather than lining them up in assembly line fashion.

• When cold packing foods, shake the jar firmly after it is filled. This allows the food to settle and pushes out excess air.

• Don't screw the thread band too tightly when you first close the jar. Instead, tighten it after it has been processed and cooled.

• A sauce is only a step away from a jam; cook it less and process it sooner.

• Keep a stack of saucers in the freezer when making jams and jellies. Test the doneness on the cold plates by putting a teaspoonful of the jam or jelly on the plate, letting it cool, and seeing if it is the proper consistency.

• When lifting jars from a water bath, hold the tongs in one hand and a folded kitchen towel in the other. Lift the jar out of the water and onto the towel. Then carry it to the counter. Many jars have been saved from breakage by this careful approach.

• Relax, take your time, and enjoy the results.

Perfect Presentation

Homemade preserves are among the most greatly appreciated and highly valued gifts. Even if you present them in a simple Ball or Mason jar with a plain label and wrapped in a brown paper bag, the thanks you receive is genuine; preserves are truly a gift in and of themselves. But we can do better than a brown paper bag. With ingenuity, little effort, and not too much money, the outside of the jar can reflect the perfection of the contents within.

Provided in the following sections are ideas for the gracious presentation of your preserves. Use the suggestions offered or develop ideas of your own. Also provided is a small source list (page 69) to help you find vendors of labels, fabric covers, and containers for your gifts.

JARS

For the recipes in this book I take a utilitarian approach and suggest the use of standard jars. They are easily obtained, convenient to use, and there is little worry about getting an airtight seal.

You can, if you have the time to hunt in specialty stores, find standard jars that have already been decorated. Generally the lids are painted with flower or fruit designs, although I have heard of jars that have been stenciled with designs using indelible ink.

European dome jars are an interesting alternative to the American standards. These jars are sealed using a rubber ring and wire clamp. Truthfully, these are tricky to use so I suggest you follow the manufacturer's instructions to ensure safe sealing and preserving.

The best time, by far, to decorate your jars is after the preserving has been done. Below are some suggestions for the decoration of your jars.

- Use attractive and decorative labels to identify the contents.

- Cut or buy attractive fabric circles (crocheted lace is a good choice) and cover the top of each jar. Tie a length of ribbon, raffia, or gold or silver elastic around the lid in a generous bow to secure the fabric.

- Decorate the lids by gluing on dried flowers, small shells, or any other naturals you might have on hand.

- Cut small hearts, stars, or other decorative shapes out of colorful, adhesive-backed paper and apply them to your jar.

- If you have a large square or circle of crocheted lace, weave a ribbon around the edge of it. Stand your jar in the circle of the lace and bring the fabric up over the jar. Pull the ribbon tightly to create a pouch; tie a bow with the trailing ends of the ribbon.

Gift Wrapping

Once the jar has been decorated, it should clearly be presented in something other than the abovementioned brown paper bag.

- Stand the jar in the center of a large square of wrapping or colored cellophane paper. Bring the ends up over the jar and twist. Tie a ribbon or decorative cord into a bow around the twist. Fluff out the ends of the paper above the bow.

- Wrap your jars in colored tissue paper and place in a foil bag. Tie the bag shut with a bow.

- Wrap the jars in tissue paper that has been decorated with glitter (white glue, which dries clear, is ideal for this) and place in a decorated gift bag.

- Line the interior of an attractive basket with a large piece of decorative fabric or a new dish towel. Place preserve jars and assorted naturals (or other embellishments) in the basket.

- Place an assortment of half-pint preserves in a decorative box and tie an embroidered or designed ribbon around it.

Shipping

In a perfect world the ideal method for packing would be to wrap each jar with bubble wrap and place it in a sturdy box, two inches apart from its neighbors, surrounded by foam popcorn or pellets. More realistically, consideration for both your pocketbook and the environment demands alternative shipping methods.

- Wrap each jar in wrapping paper and then in newspaper, cushioning it well. The wrapping paper protects the labels and fabric covers from being smudged with newsprint; you can use paper towel or tissue paper in its place.

- Place the wrapped jars in a sturdy box (I save boxes and recycle them) that has been lined with crushed newspapers or recycled foam pellets. Lay the jars two inches apart, filling the spaces with crushed newspapers or pellets. Cover the packed jars with more crushed newspapers or recycled foam pellets (or popped corn) until the box is firmly packed and the contents don't shift. Seal, label, and mail.

A word of caution about shipping your preserves: it is best not to send them during the dead heat of summer. Languishing in trucks where the temperatures can become incredibly high may cause some of the tops to pop and the jellies to loosen.

CHAPTER TWO

Jams, Jellies, and More

Imagine how delicious it would be to spread your own Ruby Red Grapefruit Marmalade on hot, buttered biscuits! This is the reason we make jams, jellies, preserves, marmalades, and fruit butters: to please ourselves and those we care for by combining fruit, sugar, and pectin (either natural or manufactured). These ingredients, with the sometime addition of an acid such as lemon juice, vegetables such as green peppers, and herbs, form the base for all the recipes listed in this chapter. The only real difference between these spreads is their textures.

• Jams are made from crushed, mashed, or chopped fruit, which is cooked with sugar until a thick consistency is reached. Manufactured pectin can be added to jam (following instructions on the container) to speed up the jelling process. Jams with pectin added need be cooked only a small amount of time (short boil). However, if you prefer to omit adding pectin, as I usually do, the introduction of lemon juice (or another acid) will enhance and bring out the fruit's natural pectin. Fruit cooked without added pectin will take longer to gel (long boil).

• Preserves differ from jams in one aspect only. The fruit is not crushed or mashed and retains much of its original shape.

• Marmalades are usually made from citrus fruit, but can also be made from other kinds of fruit, or even vegetables. The main difference between marmalade and jam is that the peel and pith are used in making marmalade. This use of the skin makes it unnecessary to add pectin and causes the slightly bitter taste for which marmalades are known.

• Fruit butters are simply fruit purees. Generally made from fruit that is high in natural pectin, such as pears and apples, the fruit and sugar are cooked slowly until a glossy, thick consistency is reached.

• Jellies are clear, gelatinous spreads that are made from the juice of fruit or infusions of vegetables and herbs. Added pectin is a must when making jellies.

The rule of thumb when making jam is three quarters of a cup sugar for each cup fruit. Honey, maple syrup, and brown sugar can be substituted when making jams, preserves, and butters but should always be done so in conjunction with granulated sugar. You can safely substitute one-half the sugar in a recipe with honey and one-quarter the amount with maple syrup. Brown sugar, which I enjoy using because of its richness, can be substituted in equal amounts, but the cups must be packed.

Spices have been paired with fruit for centuries, and touches of them in your preserves can provide both fragrance and a wonderful taste. However, when adding spices, it is best to use only small amounts, for too much of them can overwhelm the delicate flavor of cooked fruit.

All the recipes in this chapter are processed by the open-kettle/inversion method (page 10). Should you wish, they can be processed in a water bath (page 10) for approximately 10 to 15 minutes.

Strawberry-Peach Jam

Makes approximately 3 pints or 6 half-pints

2 *quarts fresh, ripe strawberries, washed, hulled, and sliced in half*

4 *cups fresh peaches, peeled, pitted, and sliced (approximately 1 pound unprocessed)*

Juice of 1 lemon

3 *cups granulated sugar*

1 *cup packed light brown sugar*

½ *teaspoon cinnamon*

Place the fruit in a large pot. Stir in the lemon juice. Heat the fruit over medium heat until it begins to soften (approximately 10 minutes). Mash the softened fruit and add the sugars. Bring the mixture to a boil and let it continue to cook until thick (approximately 25 to 30 minutes) or until it reaches 221° Fahrenheit on a candy thermometer. Watch your jam carefully and stir often to make sure it doesn't scorch. If you're worried or think you can smell the mixture starting to burn, turn the heat down and cook more slowly until the jam tests done. Testing can be done by dipping a spoonful of the hot jam onto a china or glass plate that has been kept in the freezer. Give the jam on the plate a moment or so to cool and then see if it's gelling to your satisfaction.

When the jam is ready, stir in the cinnamon and remove the pot from the heat. Let it sit for 5 minutes, then skim off all the foam. Ladle the jam into clean, hot jars, leaving ½ inch headroom. Wipe the rims clean and adjust the lids. Turn the jars of jam over and let them sit, inverted, for 10 minutes. Restore the jars to an upright position and let them cool completely. Check the seals. Label and store in a cool, dry place for up to 1 year.

Strawberry Jam

Makes approximately 5 half-pints

8 *cups fresh strawberries, hulled, washed,
    and cut in half*

Juice of 1 lemon

7 *cups sugar*

Place the strawberries in a large stainless steel pan. Add the lemon juice. Heat over a medium flame until the berries begin to soften (approximately 10 minutes). Stir in the sugar and bring the mixture to a boil. Cook, stirring con-

stantly, until the jam is thick or reaches 221° Fahrenheit on a candy thermometer (approximately 20 to 30 minutes). Skim off any foam and ladle the jam into clean, hot, sterilized jars, leaving ½ inch headroom. Wipe the rims clean and seal. Invert the jars for 10 minutes. Restore the jars to an upright position and cool. Check jar seals and store for up to 1 year.

Strawberry Rhubarb Jam

Makes approximately 6 half-pints

1 *pound rhubarb*

5 *cups fresh strawberries, hulled, washed,
    and cut in half*

Juice of 1 lemon

6½ *cups sugar*

½ *teaspoon cinnamon*

Wash the rhubarb and cut off the ends. Slice each stalk in half, lengthwise, and cut each half into ½-inch pieces. Place in a large stainless steel pan along with the strawberries and lemon. Cook over medium heat for 10 minutes or until the fruit has softened. Stir in the sugar and bring the mixture to a boil. Cook, stirring constantly, until the jam has thickened and reaches 221° Fahrenheit on a candy thermometer (approximately 20 to 25 minutes). Stir in the cinnamon until well combined. Remove any foam from the top of the jam. Ladle jam into clean, hot, sterilized jars, leaving ½ inch headroom. Wipe the rims clean and seal. Invert the jars for 10 minutes and restore to an upright position. Cool. Check seals and store in a cool, dry place for up to 1 year.

Raspberry-Blackberry Cobbler Jam

This jam is so named because when you spread it on toast, bread, or biscuits, it tastes like fresh cobbler.

Makes approximately 6 half-pints

5 *cups raspberries, gently rinsed*

3 *cups blackberries, gently rinsed*

    Juice of 2 small lemons

6 *cups sugar*

$1/4$ *teaspoon cinnamon*

$1/8$ *teaspoon nutmeg*

Combine all the berries and lemon juice in a large stainless steel pot. Simmer the berries until they begin to soften and a juice is formed (approximately 5 minutes). Mix in the sugar and bring to a boil. Lower the heat to medium and cook until the jam is thick and tests done (approximately 20 to 25 minutes). It is important when making this jam to stir constantly while cooking, particularly as the jam becomes done. Ladle the jam into sterilized jars, leaving $1/2$ inch headroom. Wipe the rims clean and seal. Invert the jars for 10 minutes. Restore the jars to an upright position and cool. Check the seals. Label and store in a cool, dry place for up to 1 year.

Perfectly Peach Jam

Makes approximately 4 half-pints

3 pounds fresh, ripe peaches, peeled,
   pitted, and coarsely chopped
   (approximately 6 to 8 large)

Juice of 1 lemon

5 cups sugar

$\frac{1}{2}$ teaspoon ground allspice

Place the fruit in a large pot along with lemon juice. Turn the heat on low and cook, stirring constantly to make sure the fruit doesn't stick, until the peaches soften (approximately 5 to 10 minutes). Add the sugar and bring to a boil. Cook until the jam gels (approximately 20 to 25 minutes) or registers 221° Fahrenheit on a candy thermometer. Stir in the allspice. Using a potato masher, crush the fruit. Turn off the heat and let the jam sit for 5 minutes. Skim off any foam and ladle the jam into clean, hot jars, leaving $\frac{1}{2}$ inch headroom. Wipe the rims clean and seal. Invert the jars for 10 minutes and then return to an upright position. Let the jars cool. Check the seals. Label and store in a cool, dry place for up to 1 year.

Black Currant Jam

Makes approximately 4 half-pints

*6 1/2 cups whole black currants
(red currants can also be used)*

1 tablespoon fresh lemon juice

5 cups sugar

Combine the currants, lemon juice, and 3 cups sugar in a large pan and bring to a boil. Cook for 5 minutes, stirring constantly. Remove the pan from the heat and let it stand, covered, for 12 hours. Return the pan to the heat along with the remaining sugar. Let cook, stirring constantly, until the jam is thick (approximately 30 minutes). Ladle into clean, hot jars, leaving 1/2 inch headroom. Wipe the rims clean, seal, and invert the jars for 10 minutes. Restore the jars to an upright position and let cool. Check the seals. Label and store in a cool, dry place for up to 1 year.

Blueberry Cassis Preserves

Makes approximately 4 half-pints

2 pints blueberries

Juice of 1 lemon

4 cups sugar

1/2 cup creme of cassis

1/2 teaspoon ground allspice

Pick over the blueberries, removing all stems, leaves, and spoiled berries. Wash the berries and place them and the

lemon juice in a large stainless steel pot. Cook the berries over medium heat until they begin to soften (approximately 3 to 5 minutes). Add the sugar and bring to a boil. Cook for 10 minutes, stirring constantly. Mix in the cassis and allspice and cook for an additional 5 minutes or until the preserves thicken and reach 221° Fahrenheit on a candy thermometer. Ladle the preserves into clean, hot, sterilized jars, leaving 1/2 inch headroom. Wipe the rims clean and seal. Invert the jars for 10 minutes. Restore the jars to an upright position. Cool. Check seals and store in a cool, dry place for up to 1 year.

Pineapple Preserves

Makes approximately 4 half-pints

2 *medium pineapples*

3 *cups water*

3 *cups sugar*

$\frac{1}{4}$ *cup lime juice*

$\frac{3}{4}$ *teaspoon ground ginger*

$\frac{1}{2}$ *teaspoon cinnamon*

Cut off the tops, bottoms, and skins of the pineapples. Make sure you remove all the eyes. Cut the fruit away from the core and dice the pineapple into small pieces. Place the pineapple in a large pot along with the water, sugar, and lime juice. Bring to a boil. Cook for 10 minutes. Add the spices. Continue cooking until the preserves have thickened and test done (approximately 20 to 30 minutes). Ladle the preserves into clean, hot jars, leaving $\frac{1}{2}$ inch headroom. Wipe the rims clean and seal. Invert the jars for 10 minutes. Restore the jars to an upright position. Cool. Check seals and store in a cool, dry place for up to 1 year.

Black Cherry Preserves

Makes approximately 4 half-pints

4 *cups Bing cherries, washed, stems removed, and pitted*

Juice of 1 lemon

1 *box powdered pectin (1$\frac{3}{4}$ ounces)*

3 *cups sugar*

Combine the cherries and lemon juice in a large pot. Heat over medium heat until the fruit begins to soften (approximately 5 minutes). Mix in the pectin and bring to a boil. Mix in the sugar, stir until it is dissolved, and again bring to a boil. Cook for 1 minute. Pour into clean, hot jars, leaving $\frac{1}{2}$ inch headroom. Wipe the rims clean and seal. Invert for 10 minutes. Restore to an upright position and cool. Check the seals, label, and store in a cool, dry place for up to 1 year.

J.C.'s Pumpkin Marmalade

Makes approximately 6 half-pints

6 lemons

*1 small pumpkin, peeled, seeded, and cut
   into ¹/₂-inch squares*

2 tablespoons fresh ginger, grated

1 cup sugar for each cup pumpkin

¹/₂ teaspoon ground allspice

Juice the lemons, reserving the rind. Place the lemon juice, pumpkin pieces, ginger, and sugar in a bowl (preferably glass or china). Toss to combine. Cover tightly and let sit for 12 hours.

Meanwhile, coarsely chop the reserved lemon rind and place in a saucepan with enough water to cover. Bring to a boil and cook for 15 minutes. Drain and refrigerate until ready for use.

Put the pumpkin mixture into a large pan and cook over medium heat until the pumpkin pieces are translucent (approximately 30 to 40 minutes). Remove the pumpkin pieces and set aside while the syrup continues to cook. When the syrup is thick, add the pumpkin pieces and lemon rind to the mixture. Bring to a boil and cook until thick (approximately 5 minutes). Ladle the marmalade into clean, hot jars, leaving ¹/₂ inch headroom. Clean the rims. Seal and invert for 10 minutes. Return the jars to an upright position and cool. Check the seals. Label and store in a cool, dry place for up to 1 year.

Ruby Red Grapefruit Marmalade

Makes approximately 4 pints or 8 half-pints

3 medium ruby red grapefruits, scrubbed

6 cups water

7 cups sugar

Cut off and discard both ends of each grapefruit along with any pits you may find. Quarter each grapefruit and thinly slice each quarter crosswise. Measure the cut-up fruit. You should have 6 cups. (If you have more, increase the water measurement by an equal amount.) Put the fruit and water in a large pan and bring to a boil. Turn the heat down and simmer for 10 minutes. Remove the pan from the heat, cover, and let the mixture sit for 24 hours. Again bring the fruit to a boil, turn the heat down, and simmer for 10 minutes. Remove the pan from the heat, cover, and let the mixture sit for an additional 12 to 18 hours. Measure the fruit and liquid. You should have 7 cups. (If you have more, increase the sugar by an equal amount.) Add the sugar to the pan and bring to a boil. Turn the heat down to medium and cook the marmalade until it gels (approximately 30 to 45 minutes) or registers 221° Fahrenheit on a candy thermometer. Ladle the marmalade into clean, hot jars, leaving $\frac{1}{2}$ inch headroom. Wipe the rims with a clean, damp cloth. Seal and process in a water bath for 10 minutes. Remove the jars, invert for 10 minutes, restore to an upright position, and cool. Check the seals. Label and store in a cool, dry place for up to 1 year.

Plum Butter

This recipe, and the one that follows, can be processed using the open-kettle method (see page 10). But as fruit butters cool rapidly, you would have to work fast. If you'd rather not risk it, process as suggested in the recipe.

Makes approximately 3 half-pints

4 *pounds medium plums*

2 *cups sugar*

$\frac{1}{4}$ *teaspoon cinnamon*

Wash the plums. Peel them by immersing them in boiling water for 45 seconds. Remove the plums from the pan and plunge them into cold water. You should be able to easily remove the skin either with your fingers or with the use of a sharp paring knife. Quarter each plum, removing the pit in the process, and place the fruit in a food processor.

Puree. You should end up with 4 cups pulp. (If you have more, increase the amount of sugar used by $\frac{1}{2}$ cup for every extra cup fruit.) Combine the plums, sugar, and cinnamon in a heavy pot or large saucepan. Bring the mixture to a boil. Turn the heat down and simmer the butter until it is thick and glossy and coats the back of a spoon (approximately 30 to 35 minutes). It will be necessary for you to stir the mixture constantly while it is cooking, for butters are so thick that they scorch easily if left unattended.

Pour the hot plum butter into hot, sterilized jars, leaving $\frac{1}{2}$ inch headroom. Seal the jars and process in a hot water bath for 10 minutes. After processing, remove the jars from the hot water and invert on clean dish towels. Let stand for 10 minutes. Restore the jars to an upright position and allow to cool. Check the seals. Label each jar and place in a cool, dry place for up to 1 year of storage or until needed for use.

Apple and Pear Butter

Makes approximately 3 half-pints

4 cups pears, peeled, cored, and coarsely
    chopped (approximately 2 pounds
    unprocessed)

4 cups Granny Smith apples, peeled, cored,
    and coarsely chopped (approximately
    $1\frac{1}{4}$ pounds)

Juice of 1 lemon

$\frac{1}{2}$ cup water

$1\frac{1}{2}$ cups granulated sugar

$\frac{1}{2}$ cup packed light brown sugar

$\frac{1}{2}$ teaspoon ground ginger

$\frac{1}{4}$ teaspoon nutmeg

Combine the pear, apple, lemon juice, and water in a large pan and cook over medium heat until soft (approximately 10 minutes). Remove the cooked fruit from the pan and puree it in a food processor. Return the fruit to the pan along with the sugars. Bring the mixture to a boil, turn the heat down, and simmer, stirring constantly, until the puree is thick and glossy (approximately 30 minutes). Add the spices and cook for an additional minute. Pour the butter into clean, hot jars, leaving $\frac{1}{2}$ inch headroom. Wipe the rims and seal the jars. Process in a water bath for 10 minutes. Remove the jars from the water bath. Invert for 10 minutes. On a clean dish towel or wire rack, restore the jars to an upright position and allow to cool. Check the seals. Label the jars and store them in a cool, dry place for up to 1 year.

Green Pepper Jelly

Makes approximately 3 half-pints

2$^1\!/_2$ cups green pepper, cored, seeded,
and finely chopped (approximately
1$^1\!/_2$ pounds)

1$^1\!/_2$ cups white vinegar

1 cup water

2$^1\!/_2$ cups sugar

1 box powdered pectin (1$^3\!/_4$ ounces)

Combine the pepper and vinegar in a saucepan and bring
to a boil. Simmer for 5 minutes. Strain the pepper through
a fine sieve or several layers of cheesecloth. Place the remaining liquid in a clean saucepan along with the 1 cup
water. Mix together $^3\!/_4$ cup sugar and the pectin and add to
the pan ingredients. Bring to a boil, stirring constantly.
Immediately add the remaining sugar. Bring to a boil again
and cook for a full minute. Remove from the heat, skim off
any foam, and ladle into clean, hot jars, leaving $^1\!/_2$ inch
headroom. Wipe the rims clean, seal, and invert for 10 minutes. Restore the jars to an upright position and cool.
Check the seals, label, and store in a cool, dry place for up
to 1 year.

Cape Cod Jelly

*A "Cape Cod" is a drink made from cranberry juice
and vodka. This jelly is a salute to the drink and
an alternative to traditional cranberry jelly.*

Makes approximately 5 half-pints

3   *cups naturally sweetened cranberry juice*

1   *cup vodka*

$^{1}/_{4}$ *cup fresh lime juice, strained*

1   *box powdered pectin ($1^{3}/_{4}$ ounces)*

3   *cups sugar*

Combine the cranberry juice, vodka, and lime juice in a
large pot. Add the pectin and bring to a boil. Boil for 1 full
minute. Ladle the jelly into clean, hot jars, leaving $^{1}/_{2}$ inch
headroom. Wipe the rims clean and seal. Invert jars for 10
minutes. Restore to an upright position. Cool. Check seals
and store in a cool, dry place for up to 1 year.

Lemon-Lime White Wine Jelly

*This jelly has a terrific kick that
makes it absolutely delicious.*

Makes approximately 3 half-pints

$^{1}/_{4}$ *cup fresh lime juice (approximately
    4 limes)*

$^{3}/_{4}$ *cup fresh lemon juice
    (approximately 6 to 8 lemons)*

$^{1}/_{2}$ *cup dry white wine*

$^{1}/_{2}$ *cup water*

3   *cups sugar*

3   *tablespoons powdered pectin*

Combine all the liquid ingredients in a saucepan. Mix $^{3}/_{4}$
cup sugar with the pectin and add to the pan. Bring to a
full boil, stirring constantly. Immediately stir in the remaining sugar. Bring to a boil again and cook the mixture for a
full minute. Remove the pan from the heat and skim off
any foam. Ladle the jelly into clean, hot jars, leaving $^{1}/_{2}$ inch
headroom. Wipe the rims clean and seal. Invert the jars for
10 minutes. Restore to an upright position and cool. Check
the seals, then label the jars and store them in a cool, dry
place for up to 1 year.

Rosemary-Thyme Jelly

Makes approximately 3 half-pints

¹/₂ cup packed fresh rosemary

¹/₂ cup packed fresh thyme

1¹/₂ cups boiling water

¹/₂ cup white vinegar

3 cups sugar

1 box powdered pectin (1³/₄ ounces)

Place the herbs in a glass or stainless steel bowl. Pour in the boiling water. Cover and let sit for 30 minutes. Strain the herb infusion through several layers of cheesecloth or a fine sieve. Place the liquid in a saucepan along with the vinegar. Mix ³/₄ cup sugar with the pectin and add to the liquid. Bring to a boil, stirring constantly. Immediately mix in the remaining sugar, bring to a boil again, and cook for a full minute. Remove from the heat and skim off any foam. Ladle the jelly into clean, hot jars, leaving ¹/₂ inch headroom. Wipe the rims clean. Seal and invert the jars for 10 minutes. Restore the jars to an upright position and cool. Check the seals, label, and store in a cool, dry place for up to 1 year.

CHAPTER THREE

Whole Fruit

It is not, as I've said before, necessary to preserve fruit (and vegetables) for the sake of survival. Grocery stores preserve all manner of these for us in their freezer sections. Furthermore, ever-increasing shipments of produce from distant lands are helping to promote the availability of fresh fruit (and vegetables) year-round. Nevertheless, I still can whole fruit, including tomatoes. The reason is simple. I like to. I like taking fruit when it's at its peak and combining it with syrups and spices to create a taste sensation that can be served with meats or poultry or as a dessert.

I especially like to preserve tomatoes because I use a lot of them throughout the year, in spaghetti sauce, casseroles, stews, and soups. I find I much prefer to open a jar of my own tailor-made tomatoes to opening a factory-processed can.

In this chapter I give you my favorite recipes for fruit. For your convenience, I give the amounts per quart or pint. This allows you to determine the quantity you make. Simply double, treble, or similarly increase the amount of liquid you will need to pour over the jarred fruit. Whereas in mixed batches, such as jam, doubling the amount is discouraged, you will not find it a problem here.

Remember, for proper processing, all the preserves in this chapter must be surrounded by some kind of hot liquid (usually water or syrup) and processed in a water bath for the amount of time stated in the recipe. Place the jars (one batch at a time) in a water bath or large pot that con-

tains warm water. Make sure there are two to three inches of water covering the lids of the jars. Bring the water to a boil and start counting off your processing time. Remove the processed jars from the water bath and place on dish towels or wire racks, inverted, for 10 minutes. Restore the jars to an upright position. Cool. Check the seals. Label and store in a cool, dry place for up to one year.

Tipsy Pears

For this recipe, you'll find it best to use Seckel, Forelli, or any other small pear. They are quite tiny and allow you to get 4 to 6 whole fruits in a jar.

For each quart:

4 to 6 small pears

2 cups water

1 cup sugar

¼ cup cognac or pear liqueur

1 cinnamon stick

6 whole cloves

Remove the buds and stem from each pear and wash the fruit thoroughly. Combine the water, sugar, and cognac in a saucepan and cook until the sugar is melted and a syrup is formed. Add the pears to the liquid and let them simmer for 10 minutes, turning the fruit from time to time to ensure even cooking. Place the cinnamon stick and cloves in the bottom of a clean, hot quart jar, followed by the pears, pushing firmly as you do so. Pour in the hot syrup, leaving ¼ inch headroom. Run a spatula around the edge of the fruit to remove air bubbles. Wipe the rims with a clean, damp cloth and place the lids. Process in a water bath for 20 minutes. Remove the processed jars from the water bath and place on dish towels or wire racks, inverted, for 10 minutes. Restore the jars to an upright position. Cool. Check the seals. Label and store in a cool, dry place for up to 1 year.

Christmas Clementines

Available from Thanksgiving to the beginning of March, clementines are a lot like tangerines, but smaller and pitless. These little darlings have a wonderful, sweet taste that is enhanced when you preserve them with spices and syrup. I love serving them during the holidays, surrounding a ham or with scoops of vanilla ice cream.

For each quart:

5 to 6 clementines
(the quantity used will depend on the size)

6 cups water

Whole cloves

1½ cups sugar

1 cinnamon stick

Remove the buds from each end of each piece of fruit. Wash the fruit thoroughly. Using a fork, prick the fruit twice, once on each side. Place the clementines in a saucepan with the water. Bring to a boil. Turn the heat down and simmer for 20 minutes. Remove the fruit, leaving the liquid in the pan, and rinse under cold water. Stick a whole clove in each end of the fruit (from where you removed the buds) and place aside.

Mix the sugar with 2 cups reserved liquid in the saucepan. Bring mixture to a boil and cook until the sugar is dissolved. Place the cinnamon stick in a clean, hot quart jar. Add the clementines to the jar. Don't be afraid to push as you put them in. Pour in the liquid, leaving ¼ inch headroom. Run a spatula around the edge of the fruit to remove air bubbles. Wipe the rims clean and seal with the lids.

Process in a water bath for 20 minutes. Remove the jars from the water bath and place on dish towels or wire racks, inverted, for 10 minutes. Restore the jars to an upright position. Cool. Check the seals. Label and store in a cool, dry place for up to 1 year.

Spiced Peaches

For each quart:

4 to 6 medium slightly ripe peaches

1½ cups water

1½ cups sugar

1 cinnamon stick

1 1-inch piece fresh ginger, peeled

Whole cloves

Prick each peach on each side with a fork to prevent them from bursting during processing. Immerse the peaches in boiling water for 3 to 5 minutes. Rinse under cold water and drain. Combine the 1½ cups water and sugar in a saucepan and bring to a boil. Cook until the sugar is dissolved. Place the cinnamon stick and ginger in a sterilized quart jar. Push a clove into the top and bottom of each peach and place as many peaches in the jar as possible. Push the fruit gently to create more room. Fill the jar with the hot syrup, leaving ¼ inch headroom. Process in a water bath for 20 minutes. Remove the jars from the water bath and place on dish towels or wire racks, inverted, for 10 minutes. Restore the jars to an upright position. Cool. Check the seals. Label and store in a cool, dry place for up to 1 year.

Spicy Cherries

For each pint:

2 cups packed firm Bing cherries, washed
and stems removed

$\frac{1}{2}$ cinnamon stick

$\frac{1}{4}$ teaspoon whole cloves

$\frac{1}{4}$ cup water

$\frac{1}{2}$ cup sugar

$\frac{1}{4}$ cup kirsch

Pack the cherries into a clean, hot jar along with the cinnamon and cloves. Combine the remaining ingredients in a saucepan. Bring to a boil and cook until the sugar is melted. Pour the hot liquid over the cherries, leaving $\frac{1}{4}$ inch headroom. Wipe the rims clean and process in a water bath for 10 minutes. Remove the jars from the water bath and place on dish towels or wire racks, inverted, for 10 minutes. Restore the jars to an upright position. Cool. Check the seals. Label and store in a cool, dry place for up to 1 year.

Peaches in Port

For each quart:

2 pounds (weight approximate)
medium peaches

Juice of 1 lemon

1 cup sugar

$\frac{3}{4}$ cup port wine

$\frac{1}{2}$ cup water

1 cinnamon stick

5 whole cloves

Peel the peaches and cut each in half, removing the pits. Place the peaches in a bowl and sprinkle with the lemon juice. Toss to combine. Mix together the sugar, port, and water and bring to a boil. Cook until the sugar is dissolved. Place the cinnamon stick and cloves into a clean, hot jar. Pack in enough peach halves to fill the jar. Pour in the boiling liquid, leaving $\frac{1}{4}$ inch headroom. Run a spatula around the edge of the peaches to remove air bubbles. Pour in additional liquid if necessary. Wipe the rims clean and seal. Process in a water bath for 10 minutes. Remove jar from bath and invert for 10 minutes. Restore the jar to an upright position and cool. Check seals and store in a cool, dry place for up to 1 year.

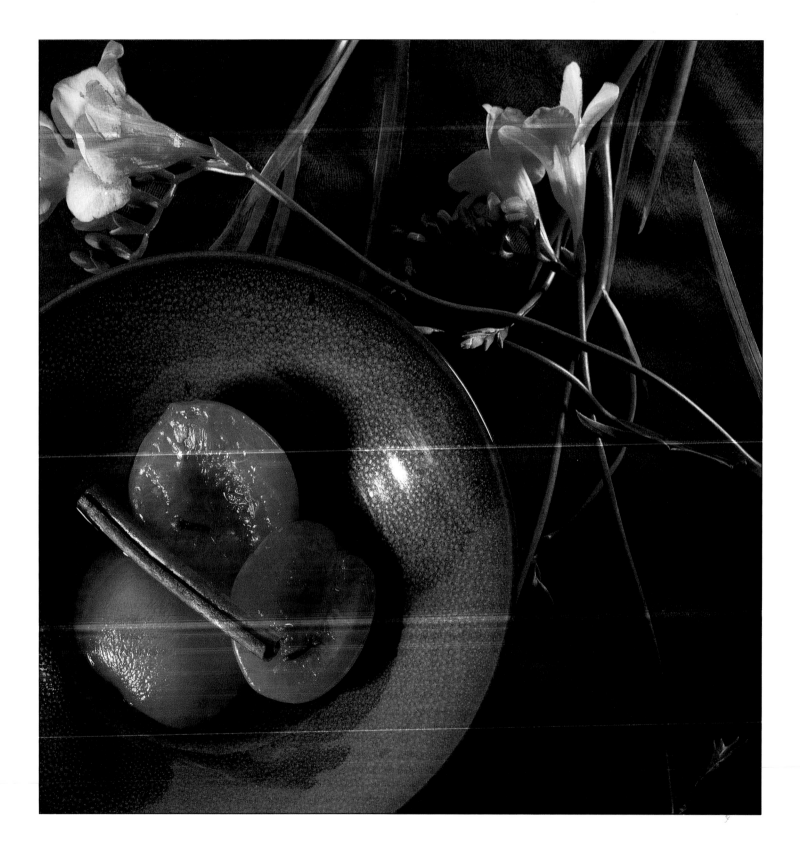

Gingered Pineapple

Makes approximately 2 pints or 4 half-pints

1 large fresh pineapple

½ cup fresh ginger, grated

2 cinnamon sticks

⅔ cup sugar

⅔ cup water

Peel, core, and cut the pineapple into large chunks. You should have 4 cups packed fruit. Divide the ginger equally among clean, hot jars. If you are canning pints, place a whole cinnamon stick in each; use ½ stick for the half-pints. Pack the fruit into the jars, dividing equally.

Combine the sugar and water in a saucepan and bring to a boil. Cook until the sugar is dissolved. Pour the hot syrup into the jars, leaving ¼ inch headroom. Run a spatula around the edge of the fruit. Wipe the rims clean. Seal and process in a water bath for 15 minutes. Remove the jars from the water bath and place on dish towels or wire racks, inverted, for 10 minutes. Restore the jars to an upright position. Cool. Check the seals. Label and store in a cool, dry place for up to 1 year.

Sicilian Blood Orange Slices

With their rich red color and sweet, sweet taste, Sicilian blood oranges are among the most wonderful of fruits. You should be able to find them at specialty shops. If not, a good substitute would be navel oranges.

For each pint:

2 *medium Sicilian blood oranges (approximately 1 pound)*

$\frac{1}{2}$ *cup sugar*

$\frac{1}{4}$ *cup Cointreau*

1 *star anise*

Scrub the oranges and place in a pot of boiling water. Blanch for 5 minutes. Remove the oranges from the pot, reserving $\frac{3}{4}$ cup liquid, and rinse under cold water. Allow the oranges to cool. Slice off the thick skin on each side of each orange and cut the remaining fruit into thin slices. Combine the reserved liquid, sugar, and Cointreau in a saucepan. Bring to a boil and simmer for 5 minutes. Place the star anise in the bottom of a clean, hot jar. Tightly pack the orange slices into the jar until you have $\frac{1}{2}$ inch headroom. Pour in the hot liquid. Run a spatula around the edge of the fruit. Gently shake the jar so that the syrup settles down onto the fruit. Pour in more liquid, if necessary, leaving $\frac{1}{4}$ inch headroom. Wipe the rims clean and seal. Process in a water bath for 15 minutes. Remove the jars from the water bath and place on dish towels or wire racks, inverted, for 10 minutes. Restore the jars to an upright position. Cool. Check the seals. Label and store in a cool, dry place for up to 1 year.

Whole Plum Tomatoes

For each pint:

5 *to 6 medium plum tomatoes (approximately 3 to 3$\frac{3}{4}$ pounds)*

1 *small clove garlic, peeled*

1 *bay leaf*

1 *tablespoon fresh lemon juice*

1 *teaspoon salt*

Boiling water

Immerse the plum tomatoes in boiling water for 2 to 3 minutes. Remove and rinse under cold water. Peel the tomatoes and cut out the bud in the top. Place the garlic clove and bay leaf in a clean, hot jar. Put the tomatoes in the jar. Don't be afraid to push; you won't do any damage, and you want the jar well packed. Sprinkle the lemon juice and salt over the tomatoes. Leaving $\frac{1}{2}$ inch headroom, fill the jar with the boiling water (approximately $\frac{1}{3}$ to $\frac{2}{3}$ cup). Run a plastic or wooden spatula around the edge of the tomatoes to remove any air bubbles. If necessary, add more water. Clean the rims and seal. Process in a water bath for 15 minutes. Remove the jars from the water bath and place on dish towels or wire racks, inverted, for 10 minutes. Restore the jars to an upright position. Cool. Check the seals. Label and store in a cool, dry place for up to 1 year.

Italian Stewed Tomatoes

Although tomatoes are an acidic fruit, adding onion and green pepper raises the pH, which would ordinarily mean that this recipe would have to be processed in a pressure canner. I get around this by adding a good measure of lemon juice. The addition of lemon allows the safe use of a water bath and adds a certain piquancy to the tomatoes.

Makes approximately 4 pints

3 *tablespoons olive oil*

2 *medium cloves garlic, peeled and minced*

1½ *cups onion, peeled and medium-diced*

1 *cup green pepper, cored, seeded, and medium-diced*

8 *cups tomato, peeled, quartered, and seeded (approximately 4 to 4½ pounds)*

½ *cup water*

⅓ *cup fresh lemon juice*

1 *teaspoon dried basil*

1 *teaspoon dried oregano*

½ *teaspoon dried rosemary*

¼ *teaspoon celery seed*

Salt and pepper to taste

Heat the olive oil in a saucepan over medium heat until hot. Add the garlic and onion. Saute until the onion is translucent. Mix in the green pepper and cook until tender (approximately 3 minutes). Add the remaining ingredients, bring to a boil, then simmer for 10 minutes. Taste the juice, adding more salt if necessary. Ladle the tomato into clean, hot jars, leaving ½ inch headroom. Run a spatula around the edge of the vegetables. Clean the rims, seal, and process in a water bath for 15 minutes. Remove the jars from the water bath and place on dish towels or wire racks, inverted, for 10 minutes. Restore the jars to an upright position. Cool. Check the seals. Label and store in a cool, dry place for up to 1 year.

When you reheat the tomatoes, add 2 tablespoons butter per pint to increase thickness.

CHAPTER FOUR

Pickles

Remember the old tongue twister that asked how many pickled peppers Peter Piper had picked? The answer is sixteen pints (uncooked). But don't worry, while I do give a recipe for pickled peppers, I don't in any way deal with such massive quantities. In fact, as in the previous chapter, I give you the recipe amounts per quart, pint, or half-pint where possible.

Pickles, either vegetable or fruit, are made with vinegar, salt, or a combination of the two, and flavored with sugar and spices. Whether whole, sliced, or cut into chunks, pickles can do more than accompany a sandwich. In this chapter I step away from standard pickles, such as sweet and dill, and give recipes for those that are more unusual but every bit as enticing. Pickled carrot sticks are wonderful on salads; pickled jalapeños give a kick to Tex-Mex and meats; pickled okra is great with bread and cheese; and pickled watermelon rind is terrific, period.

To ensure safety, pickles must be surrounded by a liquid and processed in a water bath for the required amount of time, unless stated otherwise. Remove the jars from the bath and invert on a clean dish towel or wire rack for 10 minutes. Restore the jars to an upright position and allow to cool. Check the seals, label, and store in a cool, dry place for up to one year.

Pickled Peppers

For each pint:

$^2/_3$ to 1 pound green, yellow, and red bell
    peppers, cored, seeded, and cut into
    $^1/_2$-inch strips

$^1/_4$ cup kosher salt

2 cups cold water (approximately)

$^1/_2$ cup vinegar

$^1/_2$ cup water

$^1/_4$ cup sugar

1 teaspoon pickling spice, tied in cheesecloth

1 small clove garlic, peeled

1 small dried red chili pepper

Place the pepper strips into a non-aluminum container.
Sprinkle the salt over the pepper strips and add enough of
the cold water to cover. Mix gently to dissolve the salt.
Cover and let stand for 18 to 24 hours. Rinse the strips
with cold water. Combine the vinegar, $^1/_2$ cup water, sugar,
and pickling spice in a non-aluminum pan. Bring to a boil
and simmer until the sugar is dissolved.

While the liquid is cooking, place the garlic and chili
pepper into a clean, hot jar. Pack the pepper strips into the
jar, pressing down and against the side of the jar. Remove
cheesecloth from pan. Pour in the hot liquid, leaving $^1/_4$ inch
headroom. Run a spatula around the edge of the pepper
strips. Wipe the rims clean and seal. Process in a hot water
bath for 15 minutes.

Pickled Jalapeño Peppers

For each pint:

$7^1/_2$ to 8 ounces whole jalapeño peppers, with
    stems, washed

2 cups boiling water

$^1/_2$ cup cider vinegar

$^1/_2$ cup water

$^1/_3$ cup sugar

$^1/_2$ teaspoon turmeric

$^1/_2$ teaspoon dill seed

1 clove garlic, peeled

Place the jalapeños in a colander. Pour the boiling water
over the jalapeños. Combine the vinegar, $^1/_2$ cup water,
sugar, and turmeric in a saucepan. Bring to a boil and cook
until the sugar is dissolved. Put the dill seed and garlic in a
clean, hot jar. Pack in the peppers, pushing in as many as
possible. Pour in the hot liquid, leaving $^1/_4$ inch headroom.
Wipe the rims clean and seal. Process in a water bath for
20 minutes.

Pickled Green Beans

For each pint:

$^1\!/_2$ *pound green beans (weight approximate), washed and ends snapped*

$^3\!/_4$ *cup water*

$^1\!/_2$ *cup sugar*

$^1\!/_4$ *cup apple cider vinegar*

1 *clove garlic, peeled*

$^1\!/_4$ *teaspoon dill seed*

Immerse the green beans in boiling water for 5 minutes. Refresh in cold water. Combine the water, sugar, and vinegar in a small saucepan and bring to a boil, cooking until the sugar is dissolved. Place the garlic and dill seed into a clean, hot jar. Pack the green beans into the jar. Pour in the boiling liquid, leaving $^1\!/_4$ inch headroom. Run a spatula around the edge of the beans to remove air bubbles. Pour in additional liquid if necessary. Wipe the rims clean and seal. Process in a water bath for 10 minutes. Remove from bath and invert for 10 minutes. Restore to an upright position and cool. Let the beans sit for 1 week before using.

Pickled Okra

For each pint:

$^3/_4$ cup apple cider vinegar

$^1/_2$ cup water

$^1/_3$ cup sugar

1 tablespoon kosher salt

1 dried red chili pepper

1 clove garlic, peeled

1 teaspoon dill seed

6 to 8 ounces fresh okra pods

In a saucepan, combine the vinegar, water, sugar, and salt. Bring to a boil and cook until the sugar and salt are dissolved. Place the chili pepper, garlic, and dill seed in a clean, hot jar. Pack as many okra pods as you can into the jar. Pour in the hot liquid, leaving $^1/_4$ inch headroom. Run a spatula around the edge of the okra. Wipe the rims clean, seal, and process in a water bath for 10 minutes.

Red and White Pickled Onions

For each half-pint:

$^3/_4$ cup mixed red and white pearl onions, peeled

$^1/_4$ cup water

$^1/_4$ cup apple cider vinegar

$^1/_4$ cup sugar

1 dried red chili pepper

$^1/_4$ teaspoon pickling spice

4 whole cloves

With a paring knife, cut a small crisscross in the bottom of each onion to prevent it from popping out of itself. Immerse the onions in boiling water for 3 minutes. Rinse with cool water and drain. Combine the $^1/_4$ cup water, vinegar, and sugar in a saucepan. Bring to a boil and cook until the sugar is dissolved. Place the chili pepper, pickling spice, and cloves in the bottom of a clean, hot half-pint jar. Put the onions in the jar and pour in the hot liquid, leaving $^1/_4$ inch headroom. Wipe the rims clean and seal. Process in a water bath for 15 minutes. These taste best when allowed to sit for at least 3 days.

Alice's Pickled Tomatillos

Tomatillos are known as Mexican tomatoes. Small, green, and round, they are covered with papery thin leaves that make them look somewhat prehistoric. The insides of the leaves are slightly sticky, so each tomatillo should be washed before using. They should be available in specialty shops. If not, regular green tomatoes are a good substitute.

For each pint:

$\frac{1}{2}$ cup water

$\frac{1}{2}$ cup apple cider vinegar

$\frac{1}{2}$ cup sugar

1 small clove garlic, peeled

6 whole cloves

1 teaspoon pickling spice

2 cups tomatillos, thickly sliced (approximately $\frac{1}{2}$ pound)

1 medium white onion, peeled and thinly sliced

Combine the water, vinegar, and sugar in a non-aluminum saucepan. Bring to a boil and cook until the sugar is dissolved. Place the garlic, cloves, and pickling spice in the bottom of a clean, hot jar. Layer in the tomatillos and onion, alternating the two as you go up the jar. Press down so that you can get as much in as possible and still leave $\frac{1}{2}$ inch headroom. Pour in the hot liquid, leaving $\frac{1}{4}$ inch headroom. Run a spatula around the edge of the tomatillos, thus releasing air bubbles. Wipe the rim with a clean, damp cloth. Seal the jar and process in a water bath for 15 minutes. These tomatillos taste best after being stored for at least 1 week.

Pickled Carrot Matchsticks

Makes approximately 4 half-pints

1 cup apple cider vinegar

1½ cups water

⅔ cup sugar

2 teaspoons pickling spice, tied in cheesecloth

1½ pounds carrots (approximately), peeled and washed

1 teaspoon dill seed

In a saucepan, combine the vinegar, water, sugar, and pickling spice. Bring to a boil and cook until the sugar is dissolved. Remove the pan from the heat and set aside.

Prepare the carrots by cutting them into thin, matchstick-shaped pieces approximately 3 inches long. Place ¼ teaspoon dill seed into each clean, hot jar. Fill each jar with as many matchsticks as possible. Reboil the liquid, remove the pickling spice, and pour the hot liquid over the carrots, leaving ¼ inch headroom. Wipe the rims clean, seal, and process in a water bath for 10 minutes. These should sit at least 2 weeks before using.

Mrs. Paradis' Pickled Peaches

For each quart:

4 to 6 medium, slightly ripe peaches, buds removed

Whole cloves

1½ cups packed dark brown sugar

1 cup apple cider vinegar

1½ cups water

½ teaspoon pickling spice, tied in cheesecloth

1 cinnamon stick

Immerse the peaches in boiling water for 3 minutes. Remove and rinse in cold water. Place a whole clove in the top and bottom of each peach. Set aside.

In a large pot, combine the sugar, vinegar, water, and pickling spice. Bring to a boil, then simmer for 10 minutes.

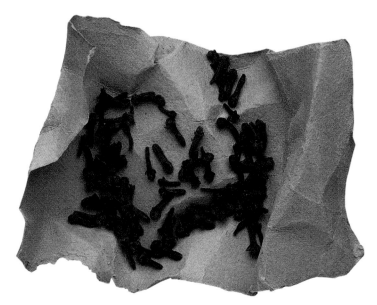

Add the peaches to the pot and cook until they begin to soften (approximately 10 to 15 minutes). Place the cinnamon stick in a clean, hot jar. Remove the pickling spice from the pot and spoon the peaches into the jar, pressing down. Ladle in enough hot liquid to leave $\frac{1}{4}$ inch headroom. Run a spatula around the edge of the peaches. Add more liquid if necessary. Wipe the rims and seal. Process in a water bath for 15 minutes. These are best when allowed to stand for 2 weeks before using.

Pickled Cherries

For each pint:

2 cups firm Bing cherries, with stems

$\frac{1}{4}$ teaspoon red pepper flakes

$\frac{1}{4}$ teaspoon coriander seed

$\frac{1}{4}$ teaspoon whole cloves

$\frac{1}{2}$ cup balsamic vinegar

3 tablespoons sugar

Boiling water

Wash the cherries with warm water and place in a clean, hot jar along with the spices. Heat the vinegar and sugar until the sugar is melted. Pour over the cherries. Pour in enough of the boiling water to fill the jar, leaving $\frac{1}{4}$ inch headroom. Run a spatula around the edge of the fruit to remove air bubbles. Wipe the rims clean, seal, and process in a water bath for 10 minutes. These are best when allowed to sit for at least 2 weeks before using.

Grandmama's Pickled Watermelon Rind

This is an old family favorite and an ecological delight. First you eat the pink fruit of the melon, then you pickle the rest. Look for a watermelon that has a good, thick rind.

Makes approximately 4 half-pints

6   *pounds watermelon (approximately 1/2 large melon)*

Water

Kosher salt

4   *cups sugar*

2   *cups apple cider vinegar*

2   *cups water*

1   *tablespoon whole cloves*

1   *tablespoon whole allspice*

1   *cinnamon stick, broken into pieces*

1   *lemon, sliced*

Remove the green skin and all the pink fruit from the rind. Cut the remaining rind into 1-inch cubes. Place the cubes in a stainless steel or glass container. Cover with the water and 2 tablespoons salt for every quart water used. Let sit for 12 to 18 hours.

Combine the sugar, vinegar, and 2 cups water in a saucepan. Tie the spices and lemon in cheesecloth and add to the pan. Bring the contents of the pan to a boil and cook for 10 minutes. Remove from the heat, cover, and let sit for 6 hours.

Drain the brine off the watermelon rind, but do not rinse. Place the rind in a large pan. Remove the spices and lemon from the syrup and pour the syrup over the rind. Bring to a boil and cook until the rind is translucent (approximately 20 to 25 minutes). Ladle the watermelon rind into clean, hot jars. Ladle syrup over the rind, leaving 1/2 inch headroom. Wipe the lids clean and seal. Invert the jars for 10 minutes. Restore to an upright position. Cool. Check the seals, label the jars, and store them in a cool, dry place for up to 1 year.

CHAPTER FIVE

Chutneys, Conserves, and Condiments

In the world of preserves, there is really very little difference between chutneys, conserves, and relishes.

Chutneys are made from a combination of chopped fruit, vegetables, spices, vinegar, sugar, and, depending on the recipe, nuts. These ingredients are cooked together until a thick jam-like consistency is reached. Fragrant as well as flavorful, chutneys are a wonderful accompaniment to curry, meats, and poultry. They also provide a nice change from pickles when serving cheese or sandwiches.

Conserves are made from at least one kind of fruit (usually raisins), nuts, and sugar. Spices are used in conserves, but in much smaller quantities than they are used in chutneys. Conserves are also cooked until a thick consistency is reached. You may find that you prefer, as I do, to cook conserves just to the point when they start to gel or hold their shape. This gives them a slightly juicy quality, which appeals to me. If you wish a firmer product, cook them as you would a jam, until 221° Fahrenheit is reached on a candy thermometer. Conserves are wonderful with poultry and some other meats and when used in desserts such as cakes and tarts.

Relishes are commonly thought of as being made from vegetables, but they can also be made from fruit. Like chutneys, relishes are made with vinegar, sugar, and spices and cooked until thick. The main difference between the two is the taste of the finished product. Relishes have a slightly sharper, more acidic taste that is often associated with pickles. Relishes will complement any sandwich, casserole, or meat dish you prepare.

Finally, you'll find recipes in this chapter for condiments that are traditional favorites, presented here with a twist. Try the blueberry catsup with a chicken burger; baste the honey mustard onto your chicken; and use the thyme vinegar in a chef's salad.

All the recipes in this chapter can be processed, unless stated otherwise, in a water bath for ten minutes or by the open-kettle method (see page 10). Remember, if there is a strange odor, any type of growth such as yeast or mold, or a fizziness when you open a jar of preserves, discard the contents immediately. Even if you are half sure that they are okay, don't chance it.

Black Cherry Chutney

Makes approximately 8 half-pints

8 cups black (or Bing) cherries, stemmed, washed, and pitted (approximately 3 pounds unprocessed)

$1\frac{1}{2}$ cups dried cherries

1 medium onion, peeled, cut in half lengthwise, and thinly sliced

3 cups naturally sweetened apple juice

$1\frac{1}{2}$ cups packed dark brown sugar

1 cup apple cider vinegar

1 tablespoon ground curry

2 teaspoons caraway seed

2 teaspoons turmeric

1 teaspoon dry mustard

$1\frac{1}{2}$ cups pecans, coarsely chopped

1 teaspoon cinnamon

In a large stainless steel pot, combine all the ingredients except the pecans and cinnamon. Bring the chutney to a boil and cook over medium heat until the chutney is thick (approximately 25 to 30 minutes). Stir in the pecans and cinnamon. Cook for an additional 5 minutes. Ladle the chutney into clean, hot jars, leaving $\frac{1}{2}$ inch headroom. Wipe the rims clean and seal. Invert the jars for 10 minutes. Restore jars to an upright position and cool. Check seals and store in a cool, dry place for up to 1 year.

Cranberry Chutney

Makes approximately 4 pints

$\frac{1}{2}$ cup dried apricots

1 cup boiling water

6 cups whole cranberries (24 ounces), picked over, bad ones removed, and rinsed in warm water

4 cups water

Juice of 2 oranges

$\frac{1}{2}$ cup orange peel, finely chopped

Juice of 1 lemon

1 cup Granny Smith apple, peeled, cored, and small-diced (approximately $\frac{1}{4}$ pound unprocessed)

$1\frac{1}{2}$ cups packed dark brown sugar

$\frac{1}{2}$ cup apple cider vinegar

$\frac{1}{4}$ cup honey

2 tablespoons curry powder

2 teaspoons salt

1 teaspoon turmeric

$\frac{1}{2}$ teaspoon ground allspice

$\frac{1}{2}$ teaspoon cinnamon

$1\frac{1}{2}$ cups toasted walnuts, finely chopped

An hour before making the chutney, cover the apricots with the boiling water. Remove the apricots, reserving the liquid, and coarsely chop the fruit. Place the cranberries,

4 cups water, and reserved liquid in a large pot and bring to a boil. Simmer until the cranberries pop (approximately 5 to 8 minutes). Add the remaining ingredients, except the walnuts, and cook over medium heat until the chutney is thick (approximately 20 to 25 minutes). Stir in the walnuts and cook until they are hot (approximately 2 minutes). Ladle the chutney into clean, hot pint jars, leaving ½ inch headroom. Clean the rims and seal. Process by the open-kettle or water bath method. Cool, check the seals, label, and store in a cool, dry place for up to 1 year.

Pear and Date Chutney

Makes approximately 5 half-pints

4 cups pear, peeled, cored, and medium-diced (approximately 2 pounds unprocessed)

1 cup onion, chopped

1 cup dates, medium-diced

2 medium cloves garlic, peeled and minced

1 cup water

1 cup packed light brown sugar

1 teaspoon dried thyme

½ teaspoon celery seed

¼ teaspoon cinnamon

Salt to taste

1 cup toasted walnuts, finely chopped

1½ teaspoons cognac or brandy (optional)

Place all the ingredients, except the salt, nuts, and cognac, in a large pan and bring to a boil. Lower the heat and simmer, stirring constantly, until the chutney is thick (approximately 20 minutes). Salt to taste. Stir in the nuts and cognac. Cook for an additional minute. Ladle the hot chutney into clean, hot jars, leaving ½ inch headroom. Wipe the rims with a clean, damp cloth. Process by either the water bath or the inversion method. Cool, check the seals, label, and store in a cool, dry place for up to 1 year.

Spicy Peach Chutney

Makes approximately 5 half-pints

3 cups peach, peeled and coarsely chopped
    (approximately $1^1/_4$ to $1^1/_2$ pounds)

1 cup red pepper, cored, seeded, and
    medium-diced

$^1/_2$ cup green pepper, cored, seeded,
    and medium-diced

1 medium onion, peeled and medium-diced

1 jalapeño pepper, stem removed,
    seeded, and minced

$1^1/_2$ cups water

$^1/_2$ cup packed light brown sugar

$^1/_2$ cup apple cider vinegar

1 teaspoon curry powder

$^1/_2$ teaspoon paprika

$^1/_4$ teaspoon celery seed

$^1/_4$ teaspoon turmeric

$^1/_4$ teaspoon cumin

$^1/_4$ teaspoon ground allspice

    Salt to taste

1 cup pecans, coarsely chopped

Put the peach into a large pot. Add the remaining ingredients, except the salt and nuts. Stir and bring to a boil. Lower the temperature and simmer until the chutney is thick (approximately 20 to 25 minutes). Salt to taste and stir in the nuts. Cook for an additional minute. Ladle the chutney into clean, hot jars, leaving $^1/_2$ inch headroom. Wipe the rims with a clean, damp cloth. Seal. Process using either the water bath or open-kettle method. Cool, check the seals, label, and store in a cool, dry place for up to 1 year.

Pineapple-Apricot Conserve

This, my Hawaiian conserve, is very rich but goes wonderfully with duck, chicken, and ham.

Makes approximately 4 pints or 8 half-pints

$1\frac{1}{2}$ cups dried apricots

$2\frac{1}{2}$ cups boiling water

1 large fresh pineapple

$\frac{1}{4}$ cup fresh ginger, grated

$4\frac{1}{2}$ cups granulated sugar

$\frac{1}{2}$ cup packed light brown sugar

$\frac{1}{2}$ teaspoon cinnamon

$\frac{1}{2}$ teaspoon red pepper flakes

$1\frac{1}{2}$ cups packed coconut

1 cup toasted slivered almonds

An hour before you make the conserve, cover the apricots with the boiling water. Cut the ends off the pineapple. Remove the skin and eliminate any eyes. Discard the core and cut the pineapple into 1-inch pieces. Reserving the liquid, take the apricots from the water and cut each into 3 slices. In a large pan, combine the apricots, reserved liquid, pineapple, ginger, and sugars. Bring to a boil and cook, stirring constantly, over medium-high heat for 10 minutes. Add the spices. Continue cooking for 5 minutes. Mix in the coconut and almonds, cooking until the desired consistency is reached (approximately 5 minutes). Fill clean, hot jars, leaving $\frac{1}{2}$ inch headroom. Wipe the rims clean. Process using the open-kettle method. Cool, check the seals, label, and store in a cool, dry place for up to 1 year.

Apple Cinnamon Walnut Conserve

Makes approximately 4 pints

3 pounds Granny Smith apples, cored, peeled, and cut into 8 1-inch sections, each section quartered

4 cups apple juice

$\frac{2}{3}$ cup currants

$\frac{1}{2}$ cup shallots, finely chopped

$1\frac{1}{2}$ cups packed dark brown sugar

$\frac{1}{4}$ cup lemon juice

$1\frac{1}{2}$ cups walnuts, coarsely chopped

$1\frac{1}{2}$ teaspoons ground cinnamon

Place the apples in a large pot along with the apple juice, currants, shallots, brown sugar, and lemon juice. Bring to a

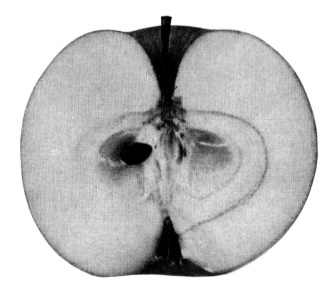

boil. Turn the heat down to medium and cook until the apples are tender and the mixture has thickened (approximately 15 to 20 minutes). Stir in the walnuts and cinnamon and cook for an additional 3 minutes. Ladle the conserve into clean, hot jars, leaving $\frac{1}{2}$ inch headroom. Wipe the rims clean and seal. Process in a water bath for 10 minutes. Remove jars from bath and invert for 10 minutes. Restore jars to an upright position. Cool. Check seals and store in a cool, dry place for up to 1 year.

Mrs. Pool's Basil Conserve

Makes approximately 4 half-pints

4 cups (approximately) green tomato, chopped

3 cups fresh basil, chopped

1 cup dry white wine

1 whole lime, bud removed, seeded, and chopped

3 cups sugar

1 tablespoon kosher salt

$1\frac{1}{2}$ cups toasted pine nuts

Combine all the ingredients, except the pine nuts, in a large pot and bring to a boil. Lower the heat and simmer, stirring frequently, until the mixture begins to thicken (approximately 25 to 30 minutes). Stir in the pine nuts. Ladle the conserve into clean, hot jars, leaving $\frac{1}{2}$ inch headroom. Wipe the lids clean, seal, and invert for 10 minutes. Restore the jars to an upright position. Cool. Check the seals, label, and store in a cool, dry place for up to 1 year.

Fig and Walnut Conserve

Makes approximately 5 half-pints

1 cup packed Sunkist figlets (or any tiny black figs)

3 cups boiling water

1 cup packed California figs (medium, light brown figs)

1 medium juice orange

Juice of 1 lemon

2 cups packed light brown sugar

1 cup water

½ cup white wine

⅓ cup cider vinegar

1½ cups toasted walnuts

1 teaspoon ground sage

Snip the stems off the figlets and place in a large bowl along with the boiling water for 30 minutes. Slice the California figs in half and place in a large pan along with the figlets and fig water. Cut the orange in half; juice half and dice the remaining half, including rind, into small pieces. Add the orange juice and orange peel to the pan. Mix in the remaining ingredients, except the walnuts and sage. Bring the mixture to a boil and cook for 5 minutes. Mix in the walnuts and sage and cook for an additional 10 minutes. Spoon the figs and walnuts into clean, hot jars, pressing down. Ladle the juice over the fruit, leaving ½ inch headroom. Wipe the rims clean and seal. Invert the jars for 10 minutes. Restore to an upright position and cool. Check the seals, label, and store in a cool, dry place for up to 1 year.

Corn Relish

Makes approximately 6 half-pints

4 cups corn kernels (either cut fresh from cob or frozen, thawed)

1 large onion, peeled and small-diced

3 medium scallions, trimmed, peeled, washed, and thinly sliced

1 large red pepper, washed, cored, seeded, and medium-diced

1 medium green pepper, washed, cored, seeded, and medium-diced

4 cups water

1 cup apple cider vinegar

1 cup sugar

2 teaspoons celery seed

1½ teaspoons turmeric

1½ teaspoons dry mustard

1 teaspoon paprika

2 tablespoons cornstarch mixed with 4 tablespoons water

In a large stainless steel pot, combine all the ingredients, except the cornstarch, and bring to a boil. Simmer for 15 minutes. Stir in the cornstarch and cook for an additional 10 minutes or until there is only a thin layer of liquid covering the top of the corn. Ladle the relish into clean, hot jars, leaving ½ inch headroom. Wipe the rims clean and seal. Process in a water bath for 10 minutes. Remove the jars from the bath. Carefully invert the jars for 10 minutes. Restore the jars to an upright position and cool. Check seals and store in a cool, dry place for up to 1 year.

Gran's Cucumber Relish

This is a wonderful turn-of-the-century relish that is so good you won't be able to stop eating it. And while it's called a relish, the flour gives it an unusual consistency. It's spreadable, making it easy to use on sandwiches, burgers, and hot dogs, while also thick enough to be served as a condiment for meats and poultry.

Makes approximately 4 pints or 8 half-pints

6 Kirby cucumbers (1¼ pounds), washed, seeded, and cut into chunks

1½ pounds green peppers, washed, cored, and seeded

1½ pounds red peppers, washed, cored, and seeded

3 large onions, peeled and cut into quarters

2 cups celery

½ cup kosher salt

4 cups sugar

1 cup flour

2 tablespoons dry mustard

2 tablespoons turmeric

2 tablespoons celery seed

2 cups apple cider vinegar

2 cups water

Using a food processor or food mill, chop the vegetables to a medium-fine texture. Place in a bowl with the salt and enough water to cover. Stir the mixture. Place a piece of plastic wrap or a plate over the bowl and let sit for $1\frac{1}{2}$ hours. Drain all the liquid off the vegetables and put them in a large pan. In a large bowl, mix together the sugar, flour, and spices. Whisk in the vinegar and 2 cups water, beating until smooth. Pour this mixture over the vegetables. Stir until well combined. Heat to boiling. Lower the heat to medium and cook the relish, stirring constantly, until it is very thick (approximately 30 minutes). Ladle the relish into clean, hot jars, leaving $\frac{1}{2}$ inch headroom. Wipe the rims clean and seal. Invert the jars for 10 minutes. Restore to an upright position and cool. Check the seals, label, and store in a cool, dry place for up to 1 year.

Red Cabbage Relish

Makes approximately 3 pints or 6 half-pints

4 cups red cabbage, finely sliced

2 cups onion, finely sliced

2 cups green tomato, finely diced

4 cups green pepper, finely chopped

$2\frac{1}{2}$ cups red pepper, finely chopped

$\frac{1}{2}$ cup kosher salt

3 cups sugar

2 cups apple cider vinegar

1 cup water

1 tablespoon dry mustard

$1\frac{1}{2}$ teaspoons celery seed

$1\frac{1}{2}$ teaspoons turmeric

In a large bowl, mix together the vegetables and salt. Cover and let sit overnight (approximately 12 to 18 hours).

Drain the vegetables well and place in a large pot along with the remaining ingredients. Bring to a boil and cook, stirring constantly, until most of the liquid has evaporated (approximately 25 to 30 minutes). Ladle the relish into clean, hot jars, leaving $\frac{1}{2}$ inch headroom. Wipe the rims clean and seal. Invert the jars for 10 minutes. Restore to an upright position and cool. Check the seals, label, and store in a cool, dry place for up to 1 year.

Onion-Pepper Relish

Makes approximately 6 half-pints

2 *pounds leek*

2 *pounds onion, peeled and quartered*

3 *large garlic cloves, peeled and halved*

1½ *pounds red pepper, cored, seeded,
    and cut into eighths*

3 *tablespoons kosher salt*

1½ *cups water*

1 *cup sugar*

¾ *cup apple cider vinegar*

1 *tablespoon ground coriander seed*

2 *teaspoons caraway seeds*

1 *teaspoon turmeric*

1 *teaspoon paprika*

½ *teaspoon crushed red pepper*

Trim the roots off the bulbs of the leeks. Cut away all but two inches of the green leaves. Slice each leek into quarters, lengthwise. Slice the quarters into ¼-inch pieces. Place the leeks into a colander and rinse thoroughly, making sure all grit is washed away. Put the leeks into a large glass or stainless steel container. Place onions, garlic, and peppers in a food processor and coarsely chop. Add the chopped vegetables to the leeks. Sprinkle salt over the contents of the bowl and mix to combine. Cover the bowl and let sit for 6 to 12 hours. Drain off all liquid completely and put the vegetables in a large stainless steel pot along with the remaining ingredients. Bring to a boil and simmer for 25 to 30 minutes or until the vegetables are tender and the relish is thick. Ladle the relish into clean, hot jars, leaving ½ inch headroom. Wipe the rims clean and seal. Process in a water bath for 10 minutes. Remove the jars from the bath. Carefully invert the jars for 10 minutes. Restore the jars to an upright position and cool. Check seals and store in a cool, dry place for up to 1 year.

Pickled Beet Relish

Makes approximately 6 half-pints

2 pounds beets, peeled and small-diced

1 large onion, peeled and medium-diced

2 medium carrots, ends removed, scrubbed, and grated

2½ cups water

1½ cups sugar

1 cup apple cider vinegar

Juice of 1 lemon

1 tablespoon kosher salt

2 teaspoons turmeric

1 teaspoon dried mint leaf

1 teaspoon ground coriander seed

½ teaspoon cumin

½ teaspoon black pepper

½ teaspoon crushed red pepper

1 tablespoon cornstarch mixed with 2 tablespoons water

Put the beets in a large pot along with the onion, carrots, and water. Bring to a boil and simmer for 30 minutes or until the beets are tender. Add the remaining ingredients (except for the cornstarch mixture) to the pot and stir to combine. Simmer for 5 minutes or until the relish has thickened. Ladle the relish into clean, hot jars, leaving ½ inch headroom. Wipe the rims clean and seal. Process in a water bath for 10 minutes. Remove the jars from the bath. Invert the jars for 10 minutes. Restore to an upright position and cool. Check seals for tightness and store in a cool, dry place for up to 1 year. Let the beets set for 2 weeks before serving them. They are delicious chilled or at room temperature.

Thyme Vinegar

I love salads, and there is nothing better on a salad than a wonderful herb or fruit vinegar. Be sure when making vinegar to use a vinegar that has 5 percent acidity. Most vinegars do, but check the front of the label to be sure.

Makes 1 pint

$\frac{1}{2}$ cup loosely packed fresh thyme

2 cups white wine vinegar

1 sprig fresh thyme

Combine the $\frac{1}{2}$ cup thyme and vinegar in a jar or bottle. Cover tightly and store in a cool, dark place for 2 weeks. Give the jar a shake every few days. After 2 weeks, strain the vinegar into a stainless steel saucepan and bring to a boil. Place the thyme sprig in a clean, hot jar. Pour the hot vinegar into the jar, leaving $\frac{1}{2}$ inch headroom. Seal, cool, and store in a cool, dark place until ready to use for up to 3 months; if at any time the vinegar becomes cloudy, discard immediately.

Orange Vinegar

Makes 1 pint

1 large orange, peeled

2 cups white wine vinegar

2 tablespoons sugar

1 strip orange peel

Cut the orange sections in half and place in a jar along with the vinegar. Cover tightly and store in a cool, dark place for 2 weeks. Give the jar a shake every few days. After 2

weeks, strain the vinegar into a stainless steel saucepan. Add the sugar and bring to a boil. Cook until the sugar is melted. Place the orange peel into a clean, hot jar and pour the vinegar over it, leaving $\frac{1}{2}$ inch headroom. Seal tightly and store in a cool, dark place until ready to use for up to 3 months; if the vinegar becomes cloudy at any point, discard immediately.

Blueberry Vinegar

Makes 2 half-pints

2 *cups white wine vinegar*

2 *cups blueberries, crushed*

3 *tablespoons sugar*

1 *strip orange peel*

Combine the vinegar and fruit in a jar. Cover tightly and store in a dark, cool place for 2 weeks. Shake the jar every few days to mix the vinegar.

After 2 weeks, strain the vinegar and combine with the sugar and orange peel in a non-aluminum saucepan. Bring to a boil. Cook, stirring constantly, until the sugar is melted. Remove the orange peel and pour the vinegar into clean, hot jars. Cover tightly, leaving $\frac{1}{2}$ inch headroom, and store in a cool, dry place for up to 1 year.

Mom's Blueberry Catsup

Makes approximately 4 half-pints

5 cups fresh blueberries

3 cups sugar

2 tablespoons fresh lemon juice

1 tablespoon cinnamon

1 teaspoon ground cloves

1 teaspoon salt, or to taste

1 teaspoon freshly ground black pepper

¾ cup Blueberry Vinegar (see page 67)

Combine all the ingredients in a non-aluminum saucepan and bring to a boil. Turn the heat down and simmer, stirring frequently, until the mixture is smooth and thick (approximately 25 to 30 minutes).

Pour the catsup into sterilized jars, leaving ½ inch headroom. Wipe the rims clean and invert for 10 minutes. Turn the jars upright and allow to cool. Check the seals, label, and store in a cool, dry place for up to 1 year.

Honey Mustard

Makes approximately 2 half-pints

½ cup dry mustard

½ cup packed dark brown sugar

½ cup apple cider vinegar

½ cup water

¼ cup mustard seed

1 teaspoon prepared horseradish

½ teaspoon curry powder

¼ teaspoon red pepper flakes

½ cup honey

In a stainless steel saucepan, mix together all the ingredients except the honey. Bring to a boil. Lower the heat and simmer for 1 minute. Pour the contents of the pan into a blender or food processor. Puree. Add the honey and pulse the machine for about 30 seconds. Pour the mustard into clean, hot jars. Wipe the rims clean and seal the jars, leaving ½ inch headroom. Cool. Store in the refrigerator for up to 3 months.

Sources

Listed below are some of the sources I have found for jars, covers, labels, baskets, and so on.

Chef's Catalog
3215 Commercial Avenue
Northbrook, IL 60062
800/338-3232

Catalog: Decorative vinegar bottles, tins, jars, decorative bottle stoppers, and cooking equipment

Dennison's

At your local stationer: Plain and bordered labels of all sizes and shapes, press-on and gummed

Gardener's Supply Company
128 Intervale Road
Burlington, VT 05401
802/863-1700
Fax 802/660-4600

Catalog: Canning equipment

Hold Everything
P.O. Box 7807
San Francisco, CA 94120
800/421-2264
Fax 415/421-5153

Catalog: Decorative seasonal tins, boxes, and baskets

Kitchen Krafts
Box 805
Mt. Laurel, NJ 08054
800/776-0575
609/778-4960

Catalog: Food preservation equipment and supplies, kitchen labels and supplies

Milan Laboratories
57 Spring Street
New York, NY 10012
212/226-4780

Brochure: Vinegar-making kits, bottles, and bottling equipment

Shaker Workshop
P.O. Box 1028
Concord, MA 01742
617/646-8985
Fax 617/648-8219

Catalog: Fine splint and reed baskets as well as wooden Shaker boxes

Smith & Hawken
25 Corte Madera
Mill Valley, CA 95941

Catalog: Terrific baskets of all shapes and sizes

Victorian Papers
Box 411332
Dept. CH 893
Kansas City, MO 64141
800/800-6647

Catalog: Lovely Victorian labels and gift bags

Williams-Sonoma
P.O. Box 7456
San Francisco, CA 94120

Catalog: Decorative cake boxes with labels, decorative waxed paper, doilies, and fine cooking equipment

Woodtown Specialties
360 E. 55th Street, Rm. 6G
New York, NY 10022
212/371-4919
Fax 212/371-4919

Brochure: Wonderfully attractive and coordinated labels, decorative gift packaging kits for canned goods, recipe cards, decorative fabric tops, and bottle bags

Index

Kitchen Metrics

The table gives approximate, rather than exact, conversions.

Spoons

$\frac{1}{4}$ teaspoon	=	1 milliliter
$\frac{1}{2}$ teaspoon	=	2 milliliters
1 teaspoon	=	5 milliliters
1 tablespoon	=	15 milliliters
2 tablespoons	=	25 milliliters
3 tablespoons	=	50 milliliters

Cups

$\frac{1}{4}$ cup	=	50 milliliters
$\frac{1}{3}$ cup	=	75 milliliters
$\frac{1}{2}$ cup	=	125 milliliters
$\frac{2}{3}$ cup	=	150 milliliters
$\frac{3}{4}$ cup	=	175 milliliters
1 cup	=	250 milliliters

Inches

1 inch	=	2.5 centimeters
2 inches	=	5 centimeters
4 inches	=	10 centimeters
9 inches	=	23 centimeters

Oven Temperatures

225F	110C	Gas $\frac{1}{4}$
250F	120C	Gas $\frac{1}{2}$
275F	140C	Gas 1
300F	150C	Gas 2
325F	160C	Gas 3
350F	180C	Gas 4
375F	190C	Gas 5
400F	200C	Gas 6
425F	220C	Gas 7
450F	230C	Gas 8
475F	240C	Gas 9
500F	260C	Gas 10

Ounces

1 ounce	=	30 grams
2 ounces	=	60 grams
3 ounces	=	90 grams
4 ounces	=	120 grams
8 ounces	=	250 grams
16 ounces	=	500 grams
2 pounds	=	1 kilogram
3 pounds	=	1.5 kilograms